GW00866559

The Fault in Our Stairs

The Fault in Our Stars Parody

By Adam Aarons

The Fault in Our Stars Parody

The Fault in Our Stairs

By Adam Aarons

PRINT EDITION v1.2c

Copyright © 2014 by Adam Aarons (mameguy@gmail.com)

All rights reserved.

This book is a work of parody and is not affiliated or associated with John Green or Penguin Group (USA) LLC.

Without limiting the rights under copyright reserved above, no part of this publication may be reproduced, stored in or introduced into a retrieval system, or transmitted, in any form, or by any means (electronic, mechanical, photocopying, recording, or otherwise) without the prior written permission of the copyright owner of this book.

Names, characters, places, brands, media, and incidents are used fictitiously. The author acknowledges the trademarked status and trademark owners of any product referenced in this work of fiction, which have been used without permission. The publication/use of these trademarks is not authorized, associated with, or sponsored by the trademark owners.

Chapter 1

Deep in the ass-end of my of my seventeenth year, my parents began to worry that I was suicidal. Perhaps it was due to my preoccupation with my own death. Or maybe, it was all the cutting. It might have been because of the time I OD'd on my pain meds—who can tell with parents? Point is, I was going to die. So what difference would it make if I got it over with it. My parents didn't see it that way and decided I was in desperate need of help. I had my choice: a shrink, or a support group.

Most people don't realize just how much Cancer sucks. It's not only the slowly dying part, it's all the sympathy too. My mom and dad were continuously worrying about me. Dad constantly crying— what a sissy! I mean, you can cry when I'm dead, man up for now.

The Cancer support group I attended (which I figured would be slightly better than having your head shrunk by a middle-aged yuppie who'd know nothing about death) was pretty terrible, thanks to all the totally gross sick people. They were all dying and boy, did it show. The group leader was a cancer survivor who milked it for all he could, running support groups as his sole means of support.

He was always talking about how we met in the Heart of Jesus—because the Church building was shaped like a cross—he said we're in the Literal Heart of Jesus.

Except that we were in the basement. I figured that's probably closer to the gut, and as I sat in the last row that put me in the ass—the Literal Ass of Jesus. No lie, there was even a basement drain right behind my seat.

At first, the meetings did give me a tiny spark of hope. My doctors had given me a ten percent chance of living. They always put it that way, not the more probable ninety percent chance of dying, but a ten percent chance of living. So that's one in ten. And guess what? There just happened to be nine other kids that attended the Cancer support group. That meant, every time one of them keeled over, I figured I was one step closer to beating the odds. If I could just knock off the others in time, I might make it. Didn't work that way though, 'cause before I could finish my internet research and plan each of their murders properly, my Cancer spread. At that point they don't say you have a zero percent chance of living, they just call it Terminal and tell you how many months, weeks, or days they guess you have left. Good news! You have 15,778,440 seconds to live—maybe less. If you break it down enough, say to nanoseconds, it almost seems like an infinity—I guess some infinities are shitter than others.

There was one cool kid in support named Isaac. I liked Isaac because his story was so unbelievably freaking sad that it made me feel better about how bad I had it. We've been friends ever since we first met.

"Hey," he'd said as he sat in the back row next to me.

"You aren't one of those Cancer Girl groupies, are you?" I asked.

"What's a Cancer groupie?" he whispered as Patrick led us in prayer.

"You know, guys who have a fetish for dying girls?" I said. "I think it's a fear of commitment. Either that or they figure dying girls are easy. You know, they'll want to get knocked up before they knock off."

"Oh," he glanced at my oxygen tank. "No, I have a girlfriend."

"What happened to your eye?" Just incase he was stupid, I pointed to his left one with a gauss pad and huge band aid over it.

3

"Eye surgery."

"Sucks."

"Yep, they took the whole damn thing."

"That's F'ed up? How'd that happen? Eye Cancer?"

"Yep. Eye Cancer."

"Don't screw with me," I scoffed. "That's not a real thing."

"I wish," he said. "It's real. What's worse is I might lose the other one too."

"Both eyes? But how?"

"STD. Caught it from a girl."

"You got an STD in your eye?"

"Yep, both of them."

"How the *Hell* does that happen?"

"Take a wild guess."

"Oh shit," I said a little too loudly. "How'd that lead to the Big C?"

"Don't know, just lucky I guess. In some people it clears up with only eye drops. Others get blisters on their eye balls and a lucky few get cancer and loose both eyes."

"Here, take my seat." I got up.

"Why?"

"Because if there's anyone who belongs in the Literal Ass of Jesus it's you."

Chapter 2

Once you get Cancer—the *I'm going to die one day* kind—you lose all your friends. Sure they still text and Facebook, maybe even come over to hang out sometimes, but no one is taking Cancer Girl and Leroy (that's the name of my oxygen tank) to the big rager on Friday night.

The only good thing is that you can guilt your ex-friends into buying you stuff. All you have to do is say something like, "Oh, I love this dress. Too bad I can't afford it. Maybe I can be buried in it," or "I *so* want to see the new Channing Tatum movie, but I don't have the money. Oh well, I might still be alive when it comes out on DVD."

That's why I hung out with Isaac; he knew what I was going through. Plus, one week he brought a totally hot guy to support group. The guy kept looking at me, so I figured he was one of those aforementioned Cancer Girl groupies—though I wasn't sure I cared.

I never spoke in group. Except I wanted to impress this boy, so I went to the front to talk about dying. "We're all dead. Some of us sooner than others. I'm basically looking out over a roomful of corpses. You're going to die. Your parents are going to die. Your sister, brother, pet turtle—all dead. Society will die out and no one will be left to give a crap. So don't feel bad that you're going first." Half the group was in tears. The other half had their jaws in their laps. "That's not just me saying it. It's from my favorite book, *A Posterior Affliction* by Peter Van Billy Bob."

Next Isaac went up and announced he was losing his other eye—that really stole my thunder.

Shortly thereafter, the meeting was over and we were evacuated from the Literal Bowels of Jesus. My mom wasn't there yet, so I watched Isaac grope his girlfriend.

Augustus walked up to me. "Hey."

"Hi," I said.

"I'm Augustus Walters."

"Hazel Mace."

"You're hot. Like Natalie Portman in *Closer*."

"Umm, I've never seen it." He was definitely a Cancer Girl groupie. "But, thanks." *Hell, who wants to die a virgin?*

"She plays a stripper."

"Okay. So, you think I look like a stripper?"

"She's a hot stripper."

I gave him a sideway glance.

"Are you friends with Isaac or Mona?" he asked, changing the subject.

"I take it Mona is the girl with Isaac's hands on her breasts?" Isaac was standing on second base and looked like he might try to seal third.

"Yep."

"He really knows how to work the Cancer sympathy card." I couldn't take my eyes off of them—it was beginning to turn pornographic. "I didn't know he had a girlfriend, what with his STD and all."

"Are you kidding?" he laughed. "She's the one who gave it to him."

"*What?*"

"Yep, best way to keep a girl from dumping you. Go down on her and get an STD in your eye, err... eyes."

"So they've done the sixty-nine thing?" I said not really surprised. I mean, given the level of affection on display right outside the Literal Heart of Jesus.

"Not quite." Augustus searched around for something in his jacket pockets. "She never returned the favor."

"Seriously?" I cried. "That's totally unfair!"

"I know," he said. "Says she's going to do it now that he's going have his other eyeball dished out, though."

"I should hope so," I said before realizing I was advocating sexual favors as a form of penance.

"Wanna to come to my place and act out my favorite scene from *Closer*?"

"I already told you, I haven't seen it."

"So we watch it first." He pulled something out of his pocket. "And you can pick your favorite scene, too"

I was considering his offer, when I saw what had in his pocket. It was a glass pipe, a crack pipe, which he filled with small white rocks right in front of me and then lit up.

"Ummm," I wasn't sure how to proceed. "Are you standing in front of a church smoking crack cocaine?"

"Oh, no," he told me. "I don't inhale."

"Excuse me?"

"Smoking crack cocaine is just about as stupid as you can get." He took a few puffs like he'd fully explained himself.

"*And*?" I shouted.

"And so, I don't actually inhale. That way, I know no matter what stupid thing I do, it'll never be the stupidest thing of all."

"*That* is the stupidest thing I have *ever* heard."

"No it's not. Smoking crack cocaine would be."

Good thing he was really hot.

I realize at this point you may be thinking the crack pipe is totally ridiculous and unbelievable. Maybe even some sort of idiotic plot device—that there's no way this kid was pretending to smoke crack. Hang in here with me on this one. It will all become clear later, I promise.

I agreed to go to Augustus' house, as long as he knew there would be *no* stripper role-playing whatsoever.

I texted my mom: *Going 2 watch movie at cute boy's house. Don't worry met him in Cancer group.*

Her reply: *OK, but use a condom. U don't want 2 end up pregnant & dying.* My mom, always looking out for me.

We got to his house, and it turned out he lived in his parent's basement. Which is a problem when you're lugging around a twenty-pound cylinder of oxygen.

"Do you want me to carry that for you, Hazel?" He reached over to pick up my tank.

"Hands off Leroy!" I slapped his hand.

"Ouch! Okay, okay." He took two steps down and turned to wait for me, probably hoping to catch a feel if I stumbled. "You named your oxygen tank?"

"Everyone does." I frowned at him and took my first hesitant step.

"Leroy?"

"It's a long story." I lifted Leroy down the first step.

"I think we have the time." He descended another step in front of me.

"Fine. When I first got my tank the guy who got me set up—you go to a medical equipment place for that, not a hospital. Anyway, the guy's name was Leroy, and he was black."

"Why'd you mention that it wasn't a hospital? You think a guy named Leroy can't work in a hospital?" He reached out a hand, which I ignored.

"Whatever." I shook my head. "I was there with my best friend Payton. She's really into black guys and said something like, 'I bet he's hung like a stallion'."

"Yes, because everyone knows all black men are hung like horses."

"Exactly. So the room's filled with oxygen cylinders, all aluminum-silvery except for one, painted black, completely black." I'd managed about three steps. "That's the one he gives me. And before the door's even closed behind him, Payton says, 'OMG, Leroy just gave you his big, black cylinder'."

At this point Augustus laughed.

"And the name stuck." We'd made it to the turn in the stairs.

"So you have a special relationship with Leroy then?"

12

"Hell no, I hate dragging him around. Now my oxygen concentrator, that's a different story—we're close."

"What's an oxygen concentrator?"

"It replaces Leroy when I sleep. It's a big box that pulls oxygen from the air." I started to lose my footing on a loose step but just managed to keep from falling.

"And you two are close?"

"It really gets vibrating when it's been on for a while." I'd made it down the last stair, and Augustus put out his hand—at that point I didn't have much of a choice but to take it.

I was having some trouble breathing, and Augustus began helping me more and more. By the time we were at the couch, I was almost in his arms and completely out of breath.

"You okay?" he asked, as his bulging, muscular arms gently sat me on the couch.

"Yep, I just need a second."

"I guess your lungs don't work so well."

"No, they're fine," I said laying back. "It's just the tumors trying to drown me by filling them up with fluid."

Chapter 3

The movie started out like a typical romantic comedy, but quickly turned into a twisted sex romp. Instead of a Love Triangle, it was more of a Love Rhombus.

Even though he'd already seen it before (several times, I gathered), he got all excited at the sexy parts. I should have been turned off, but the fact he thought I looked like Natalie Portman—a sexy Natalie Portman—meant I cut him some slack. I did really like one line in the movie, but it was one by Julia Roberts: *Men are crap*.

After the movie, Augustus tried to get under my shirt. But I still had those stairs to climb back up, and I didn't want to get worked up. So I had to squash his hopes.

After a little light petting, I told him I had to go.

"What already? The night is young."

"I don't normally sleep with boys I've just met." I started getting up.

"Neither do I, but I think I can make an exception."

"Try the Mother Lode Club," I said.

"What?"

"The Mother Lode, it's a gay bar—you said you wanted to make an exception about sleeping with boys that you've just meant. That's the place," I replied.

He knew he'd been outwitted. I let him help me up the stairs so I didn't burse his ego too badly.

He drove me home. He was a model driver—considering he had a crack pipe hanging out of his mouth.

Chapter 4

The next time I saw Augustus I brought him my copy of *A Posterior Affliction* and told him if he wanted to have any chance of deflowering me, he'd have to read it.

"I hate reading."

"I'm worth it," I simpered.

He tilted his head noncommittally.

"What do you mean, you don't read *anything*?"

"Besides *Penthouse Letters*, not a... Oh wait there *is* one."

Excitedly, he dug around the many piles of dirty clothes scattered around his room until he found it. "It's by Chuck Palahniuk. It's called, *Snuff.*"

"It's about killing?"

"Kinda," he said, "Is *A Posterior Affliction* about butt sores?"

"Kinda. But not really." He nodded.

"Does it have strippers in it?" he asked.

"No."

"Porn stars?"

I shook my head. "It's not that kind of book."

"I'll read your terrible book with the pathetic title that does not contain strippers or porn stars. But you've gotta read my book in return."

We agreed to read each other's books and compare notes. But I felt stupid because I knew he'd hate my book.

"What are all these trophies about?" I asked him as I stepped over a discarded pizza box.

"Baseball."

"I didn't know you play baseball."

"Used to," he said, "I really didn't like it."

"Why not?"

"All the butt slapping." He turned away, "Haven't you ever noticed how baseball players all spank each other on the rear?"

"Yeah, seems a little weird. But you liked *playing* the game, right?"

"I used to, then all at once, I was like, why the Hell am I rounding all these bags while my teammates and coaches are slapping my ass? It seemed like the gayest thing I could possibly be doing."

We made out for a while and I let him carry me back up the stairs. That was the first time I noticed his limp. I was surprised I hadn't noticed it sooner. It must be all the pain pills mixed with Xanax. Docs don't like to mix the two, but when you always feel like your own lungs are slowly drowning you, there's not a lot of medicine besides Xanax that can keep you from having constant panic attacks.

Chapter 5

We both went to Isaac's house the morning of his operation. When we got to the door, his Mom told us Mona had just broken up with him a few hours ago. "And that bitch never even went down on him," she added under her breath. Actually, it wasn't under her breath at all, but I think she meant it to be.

We expected him to be really upset, which he sorta was. But he was high as a kite too. His mom had already given him something to calm him down before the surgery, and it'd worked—mostly.

"I can't believe she dumped me." His head was wobbling around on his neck.

"I know, I know," Augustus said.

"She promised we'd be together. She said, 'When you give someone a STD, that's forever.' She wore it."

"She's a whore," I said, surprised at my level of pissed-atude.

"You know what the worst part is?" He was really slurring his speech now. "The worst part is, last week, Amy Green offered to let me see her rack."

"Really? Those melons are huge." Augustus sounded impressed.

"We were at Bill Spiegel's party and she came up to me and Mona, saying how sorry she is and crap. She went on about how terrible it was that I'll never see another pair of tits in my life, and right there, she offers to show me hers."

"Dude, I miss all the good parties," Augustus lamented.

"But Mona's like, 'My tits are the only ones he's ever going to touch, so they're all he needs to see'."

"Oh, man." Augustus seemed at a loss.

"One pair of tits. Is that enough to get me through an entire life?"

"No," I took off my jacket. "No, it's not." I started unbuttoning my blouse.

"Whoa," Augustus said, "Hold on now. I haven't even seen those... yet."

"You've got time. Isaac doesn't," I held my shirt closed with one hand and pointed with the other, "Augustus, turn around."

"Oh this sucks." He turned his back to us. "Can I have a peek?"

"How far are you into *A Posterior Affliction*?" I stepped towards Isaac, whose single eye bulged.

"That book is terrible! It's all about anal cancer and gardening."

I made sure Augustus wasn't peeking, then undid my bra and pulled out the twins. "Sorry, they're not as big as Amy Green's."

"Wow, they are so much better than Mona's! Her nipples are way smaller and flat, like mosquito bites compared to yours."

I blushed. "They're not that big."

"Be careful where you point them, you could poke an eye out with one of those."

There was awkward silence for a moment then we all laughed until we couldn't stand.

We promised Isaac we'd visit him in the hospital, and we both stood outside his house and cried as his mom drove him away.

"Can you believe some doctor is actually going to scoop his entire eyeball out?" Augustus wiped a tear. "It's like something that doesn't happen in real life. Like something only a really F'ed up writer would think of, like a writer who writes about really F'ed up unbelievable stuff—but nobody realizes it's not believable and so he get a movie deal and earns millions making that crap up."

We were feeling like crud, so we went to the movies. A comedy by Seth McFarland. Like most of the stuff he does, it was stupid. Augustus kept going on about not being able to see my tits, so I let him cop a feel—for about five seconds until he pinched.

"Ouch," I slapped him. "What's the matter with you?"

"That's what they do on the Internet," he said. "Sorry."

"This isn't internet porn." I put his hands back in his lap. "You don't pinch, twist, or roll them like quarters. The key is to be gentle."

"Okay, sorry," he said. "I'll do better next time. Let's go again."

"Nice try, slick."

After the movie, he drove me home with the stupid crack pipe in his mouth, and we made plans to visit Isaac.

Chapter 6

We did go and see Isaac in the hospital, but he was totally out of it. Augustus shook him and even tried to animate him like a Muppet, but he didn't wake up. I left flowers. Augustus left a balloon animal, saying since he couldn't see it, maybe he could feel it.

It was another week before either of us spoke to him. His Mom had dropped him off at Augustus's house. He wore the same sunglasses as usual, except the gauze and bandages were over the other eye now. He also carried a white cane.

Isaac cursed as he felt his way down the stairs, tripping over the loose one.

He got up and walked towards us but bumped his shin on a coffee table.

We stood there silently, not sure what to say—should we ask him if he was all right or pretend like everything was normal?

He started screaming. "That stupid bitch... Look what she did to me. She knew, but did she care? How am I'm ever going to get a girlfriend now? I'll probably never even have oral sex."

"Isaac, it's okay, let it out," I told him.

"Yeah, it's okay for dudes to cry," Augustus told him.

"Not this one," his voice cracked. "They took it all, even the tear duct. I literally can't cry."

Whoa, can't cry. There are few things better in life than a good cry. I couldn't imagine *never* being able to cry again.

"I… I just need to break something. Smash it to bits, to get my anger out."

"Isaac, use my trophies. I hate them anyway," Augustus said. "Smash them to pieces."

"Thanks, you're a real friend."

"They're right behind you. Have at it."

Isaac turned around, only he hadn't been blind for long, and when he reached over, he grabbed a lamp and smashed it on the ground.

"No, no," yelled Augustus. "That was a lamp—to your left. Left!"

As Augustus reached down for the lampshade, Isaac turned to the left. He turned too far and reached for a ceramic container alone on a shelf, and, before we had a chance to shout stop, he threw the urn containing Augustus' grandma to the floor.

Dust exploded into the room like smoke. I didn't fancy breathing anyone's dead grandma, so I made my way up the stairs as quickly as Leroy allowed. As I turned the corner landing, I saw Isaac reaching for the laptop, Augustus desperately trying to stop him.

It sounded like they were bulldozing the basement. They both came up a few minutes later. Augustus looked like he'd just corralled a bull, and Isaac's face burned red like he'd been crying—though I knew that couldn't be true.

"Get Leroy. We're leaving," Augustus announced.

I grabbed my constant companion and followed them out the door. "Where are we heading?"

"You'll see." Augustus prepped his crack pipe.

We drove in silence to an upscale part of town. Augustus pulled over between two fancy houses. "Quiet now."

I carefully shut my door and followed them to a big house with a pink convertible Cooper Mini out front. Augustus led Isaac up to the car and with his big muscular arms lifted him onto the car door's open window frame, like a dad putting a kid in a booster seat.

Isaac pulled his pants down, and his bare butt hung over the driver's seat. He strained as he made his deposit onto the driver's side seat.

"Farts demand to be passed," Augustus said, which was a line from *A Posterior Affliction*.

"It's more of a shart—pain meds give me the runs." Isaac pulled up his pants and jumped down. "It doesn't feel like enough."

"Here, let me make a contribution." Augustus climbed up onto the hood, undid his shorts, and dropped a load.

"Oh, me too." I ran round to the far side, opened the door, and pulled my pants down just enough.

"What are we waiting for?" Isaac said. "Let's get out of here."

"Hazel is pissing in Mona's car! And she's doing it standing up!"

"Damn, I want to see that," Isaac moaned. "How does a girl piss standing?"

"Practice," I said. "Augustus, stop staring."

26

"She's doing it with one hand." Augustus's eyes were fixed.

"How does that even work?" Isaac asked.

"Google it," I said as I pulled my pants back up.

A light turned on in an upstairs window. "We better get out of here." Augustus grabbed Isaac's arm and led him to the car.

"I think my sense of smell is getting better," Isaac said. "I can still smell piss and shit."

"It's not just you," I said plugging my noise as we drove off. "What did you guys eat?"

"Us? I can smell your pee from here."

"It's *my medication*," I said. "I doubt she'll be able to get the smell out of her car."

Chapter 7

I didn't see Augustus for a while, not because he wasn't trying to hit my lovely female bits, but because I had a stay at the damn hospital to get my lungs drained. They were filling up quicker each time—I could almost feel myself descending into a death spiral.

Augustus showed up the day after they started letting me have visitors.

"You're late," I said as he walked in carrying a huge bouquet of flowers and a balloon animal shaped like… I had no idea what it was shaped like.

"Sorry, I had something unexpected come up."

"Something more important than me?"

"Hey, I got you a Leroy shaped balloon."

"That's Leroy?" I asked. "It looks more like a sperm."

"That's your oxygen line. Not a tail."

"Oh."

"I've got some good news. I finished *A Posterior Affliction*."

"You did? All of it?"

"Most," he admitted. "I skipped a few pages here and there. But I got the general idea, we're all going to die—if we're lucky, it won't be from anal cancer."

"Yeah, but didn't it leave you wondering about Anna?"

"Wondering what?"

"Didn't you read any of it? Anna, the girl with anal Cancer."

"Yeah, anal cancer. That's not a real thing, right?"

"It is. Farah Fawcett had it." I was getting irritated.

"Wasn't she a porn star, like a long time ago?"

"*No!*" I yelled. "Remember Anna's Mom? She was obsessed with growing the perfect pot plant and was missing an ear from a drug deal gone bad." He nodded like he remembered, but I didn't believe him. "Don't you wonder what happened to her? Did she marry the rich Arab Oil Baron? Was he even really rich? And don't even get me started about Anna."

"She died. I mean, she dropped dead mid-sentence. The book just stops." He took out his pipe. "Who cares about the rest?"

"I do," I told him. "I'm going to die, sooner rather than later, and I want to know what happens before I go."

"Well then, Hazel Mace, I vow to find out for you."

I got out of the hospital at the end of the week, and even though I was feeling much better since I could take nice deep breaths, the doctors saw fit to put me on bed rest.

Augustus still came over every day. He even brought Isaac over once, which was terrible because Isaac was the most depressed, the most pathetic, the saddest person in the entire world.

The day after Isaac's visit, Augustus showed up with a big smile on his face.

"Wow, you look happy," I said. "Did you get laid?"

"I'm working on it." He held up a sheet of paper "Got the contact address for Peter Van Billy Bob—the author of *A Posterior Affliction*."

"What," I cried. "How? I've written his publisher like a hundred times, and they haven't replied once."

"I found his agent and wrote her directly. I have her email here."

"Let me see." I reached out for the letter.

"Now, now. We can't have you getting worked up." He pulled it away. "I'll read it to you."

"Dear Mr. Walters,

Thank you for your heartfelt email. I was troubled to hear about your girlfriend and pray for her speedy recovery (I used the cancer angle to make sure she'd write back). Unfortunately, I am unable to provide the answers to the questions she is looking for, as my relationship with Mr. Billy Bob has come to an end.

I have included his mailing address. Perhaps if you contact him directly he may reply. However, I must warn you that the commercial failure of his book has caused him great distress and that he is currently suffering from a severe addiction. I am afraid your correspondence may go unanswered.

I wish both of you the best. Sincerely,

Beth Adams

Senior Agent, The Burg Agency."

"Wow, you've got his address? Now I can write him directly."

"No, no." He shook a finger at me. "Remember our deal. I get you the answers, and you give me full access to your pants."

"My pants are not a wish granting factory."

He glanced at the letter, then down at my crotch.

"Fine. Whatever, but you've gotta get the answers, first."

Chapter 8

Several weeks went by without Augustus saying anything about the letter. Then one day, as we sat in my room (since I was less mobile now, my mom threw out the *no boys in my bedroom* rule) he pulled out a letter.

"You got it?" I jumped in my seat. "A reply!"

"No, no," he looked heartbroken. "It's another one from the agent. She said he's not even returning her calls now."

"What a jerk."

"I know. She warned us." He started picking up a notebook that I'd left on my nightstand.

"Hey, give that here." I snapped the notebook out of his hands.

"What is it, your diary?" He smirked. "I already know what it says: I'm dating this really hot guy. But I totally won't let him get past second base, even though he's a total hunk and I really should put out—but I just like giving him blue balls too much."

"Oh, very funny." I scoffed. "If you must know, it's my writing notebook."

"You write?"

"Just poetry."

"Read me some." He clasped his hands like in prayer. "Please."

"No way."

"Oh, come on I said, please," he begged. "I'll write you a poem, I promise."

"Fine, you write me a poem first, *then* I'll read you one, just one, of mine."

"It's a deal."

We made out for a little while, and, for the first time, I let him sneak past second but tagged him out short of third."

"This is too much." He was putting his shirt, which had come half way off, back on. I admired the view. "I'm going home to write that poem. It's going to be so good that you'll be overwhelmed by desire for me."

A didn't see or even hear from him for two days. Then, on the third day, he showed up with a basket in hand.

"What's this?" I asked.

"I've cleared it with your mom. Hazel Mace, I'm taking you for a picnic."

Wow, that was like the most romantic thing a guy had ever done for me. "Okay." I didn't know what else to say.

As he helped me get Leroy out the front door, Mom came over and gave me a kiss on the cheek. "Don't do anything I wouldn't do," she whispered, "if I was dying." And she discreetly slipped a condom into my hand.

Augustus managed to find the most isolated part of the most isolated park in the city. There was no grass; it was really closer to a forest than a park. He laid out a big, checkered blanket and a bucket of fried chicken.

"Wow, you really know how to go all out," I said.

"It's a hillbilly themed meal, like your favorite book. And that's not all." He reached into his back pocket and pulled out a ragged scrap of paper. "I wrote your poem."

Roses are red, girlie parts are pink

When I smelled your pee, Wow, did it stink

But if you let me in, boy, I wouldn't care

I'd just thank God I'd finally made it in there.

"That has to be the absolute worst poem in the history of poetry—even in the history of guys writing poems just to try to get laid."

"So no dice, huh?"

"I didn't say that." I pouted my lips and pulled down the lower one with a finger. I was trying to be sultry, but it's hard when you have nasal plugs and rubber tubing running to an air cylinder.

"You're just trying to get out of your end of the deal," Augustus said.

"What?"

"Your poem, you promised to read me one of yours."

"I don't have my notebook with me," I protested.

"You suck Hazel Mace. I did all this work on mine, and now you don't hold up your end of the bargain?"

"Fine. I've got one I've been working on in my pocket. But it's pretty intense."

"Intense is good." He smiled.

"Not that kind of intense." I threw a chicken leg at him. "Now, don't interrupt."

Here's the poem I read for him it's titled, *Nothing*:

Mercy looked at the gun. The bottle of pills. The razor blade. The rope. The tabletop lamp.

She picked up the razor blade.

She picked up the lamp.

She cut off the cord with the blade. Careful not to nick the copper, she separated the pair of wires. She sliced open the plastic cover.

Six months they say. If you want to die, give it six months— things get better.

They hadn't.

They wouldn't.

They couldn't.

She was broken. She couldn't feel. Not like normal people. Oh, a slice here and a slice there. A few seconds of muted pain. But you could only cut so much.

She pried the plastic sheath from the copper. The bare wires looked like pubic hair.

She put the cord down.

She pushed it out of sight.

She began to shake as she stared at the razor blade in her
other hand.

She wanted to feel.

Pain is good. Pain is the only good he remembered.

Sometimes, when her sheets ran red she'd get turned on.

Sometimes, when her head began to fade, she didn't know
why she stopped.

Sometimes, if she just sliced deep enough, she thought she'd
be normal.

She pressed the razorblade against her thigh.

She wanted to slide it up. She wanted to slice it down.

She didn't.

She ran the blade down the lampshade instead. With closed
eyes, she listened, enraptured by the snapping of each thread.

She left the blade in the shade.

She picked up the cord without turning from the blade.

She felt the metal prongs of the plug, pressed her fingers
against them until she thought she felt blood.

She looked down at her dry fingers with disappointment.

She ripped the plastic sleeve off the second wire.

She wanted something she didn't know how to get.

She wanted anything.

She sat in the dark.

Time went by.

She couldn't stand the nothingness. She wrapped the bare copper wiring around her arm, but felt nothing so she unwrapped it.

She tied the end in a loop, and with as much force as she could, pulled it taught.

She wrapped it around her arm, pulling as tight as possible—two more times around.

Her fingers tingled.

She felt it.

She continued to wrap her arm. She felt it, tighter and tighter.

She made a loop with the other wire.

She wrapped her other arm.

She could feel it.

She pulled as tight as she could.

She cursed when she couldn't get the second arm as tight as the first.

A small trickle of blood ran down the first arm.

She breathed deeply.

She looked at the cord's plug. Then the wall socket.

She would plug herself in, she thought.

One hundred and ten volts, a warm embrace.

She imagined the eager electricity, violently contracting the muscles in her arms.

In her shoulders.

In her chest.

In her Heart.

A warm embrace, how she longed for it.

She stopped—surprised by sensation.

Her hand burned.

Her fingers swelled, red as the trail of blood that dripped down them.

She sighed deeply.

The other fingers burned too.

She waited.

The burning expanded.

She grew excited.

The pain moved into her hands.

She moaned.

Up. Up into her arms it crept.

Pain. Her face cracked a smile as she waited for her arms to explode.

She sat in ecstasy—she wet her pants.

But the feeling wore off, leaving the numbness behind.

She looked at the wall socket—longed for it.

She reached for the plug.

She fumbled and dropped it.

She tried the other arm—her fingers betrayed her.

She sat, looking at the plug.

Tears rolled down her cheeks.

She cried.

Pain, hate, despair rolled over her in exquisite waves.

Oh, to feel.

A minute later it was gone. Numbness remained.

Numb fingers.

Numb hands.

Numb arms.

Numb soul.

She tried to grab the plug again—her fingers wouldn't move.

With her teeth, she ripped the cord off her right hand.

Fingers still unable to move.

With her teeth, she ripped the cord off her left hand.

She watched her arms as the blood receded—

Powerless to stop the life from seeping back into them, she

sat in the dark.

She felt nothing once more.

"That's some F'ed up crap," he said, once he was sure I was finished.

"That's the idea."

"Wow, okay." He popped open a bottle of champagne. "Let's move on then."

Augustus poured me a glass, and before I knew it, we were laying on our sides making out. I reached over and unbuttoned his

42

pants. I wasn't sure this was the right place to go all the way, but he got his pants off faster than a redneck at a swimming hole.

"Oh my gosh. What the Hell is that?" I screamed.

"What." He looked behind him, as if he wasn't taking his leg off.

"Your leg, it's wooden."

"It's a composite actually." He unstrapped it, and he held it in his hand. "I thought you knew."

"Oh no. Not the stump!" But it was too late. I'd seen it. It was all smooth, and callused, and… stumpy. "I'm sorry, but I cannot look at that thing." I got up and stepped away.

"Hazel Mace, I walk with a limp, you must have known." He stood up on one foot, his prosthetic still in hand. "It's just a stump."

I ran.

When you look like one of the walking dead dragging an O_2 cylinder around, hitchhiking is easy. I passed up two pervy old men before getting a ride with the mother of three little brats. The constant yelling was slightly better than being hit on by old dudes.

Chapter 9

When you really F up, it's hard to know how to make amends. Sex will do it. I decided to get all dolled up and go apologize to Augustus.

I did my hair up in a fancy bun, put on a thong and a sundress, made sure I had a condom in my purse and borrowed my mom's car.

Augustus' mom let me in, told me he was downstairs, and offered to help me carry Leroy. I wondered why she didn't call Augustus up.

I should have accepted her help, because I was so nervous I totally forgot about the loose step and fell down the stairs, Leroy trailing after me. Luckily, Leroy rolled to a stop next to me.

Augustus sat in an old beanbag chair on the corner. He barely looked over at me.

"Yeah, I'm fine. Thanks for your concern." I stood up and got Leroy's cart, which was still on the stairs.

"Sorry," Augustus mumbled.

"Augustus, what's wrong?" His face was bright red. He had wet, bloodshot eyes and even snot dripping down his nose.

"It's my cancer," His voice trembled. "It's back."

"How bad is it?" I raced over to him.

"Bad."

We sat around and talked for hours about his Cancer. It was bad; they were throwing the "T" word around. He'd find out in a week when the tests all came back. We talked about what an ass Peter Van Billy Bob was. And we disagreed about the literary merits of *Snuff*. We talked about the things we would never do—growing up, getting real jobs—except we talked about them like them as if they were going to happen. I'd be a vet who specialized in turtles, and he'd make a living managing Cancer support groups and giving motivational speeches to high school kids. Oh, and if you were wondering, at that point, sex was *way* off the table.

I left that night feeling as bad as the day I first got my diagnosis.

We didn't see each other for a few days. He'd already started a round of Chemo, and the first couple days are always the worst.

I hadn't talked to him in over twenty-four hours when there was a knock at my door. "Hazel, it's for you."

It was Augustus. "Hey."

"What are you doing here?" I was shocked to see him. "You should be in bed."

"With you." He smiled.

"Knock it off. I'm serious."

"I'm fine," he said. "They've got me on new pain meds."

"Then you shouldn't be driving."

"No, no I'm fine to drive. As a matter of fact, that's why I'm here."

"Why?"

"To drive you to Kentucky."

"*Where?*"

"To Peter Van Billy Bob's house. I've got the address; it's less than eight hours away. We can make it by evening."

"That's crazy," I protested.

"Maybe, but shouldn't everyone do something crazy at least once in their life?"

"My Mom will never go for it."

"She already has. I told her I'm taking you to a hotel for the evening."

"My O_2 tank only lasts like nine or ten hours."

He looked crestfallen. "Do you have a backup? Could we take your vibrating air machine?"

"If I'm sitting in your car, I can get away with cutting Leroy's O_2 level. As long as we drive straight back, I should be okay."

I quickly packed a few things and kissed my Mom goodnight. She told me, if my dad asked, to say I was at Augustus' house and not to mention a word about a hotel.

I fell asleep shortly after we hit the interstate, and I didn't wake up until Augustus stopped for gas.

"Where is this place?" I asked looking at the rundown gas station and two little kids wearing nothing but cloth diapers and a layer of dirt.

"The Appalachians. Run if you hear banjo music." Augustus started pumping gas. "Peter's house is about thirty minutes from here."

We drove through the poorest area I'd ever seen. Beautiful hills and woods marred by crumbling buildings and littered with dirty, half-clothed children.

Peter's house was off a dirt road. It was a singlewide mobile home with broken windows and a tarp over the roof. Two old trucks sat in the driveway; one was slowly being reclaimed by the forest.

"Are you sure we should do this?" I said hesitantly as we climbed the rickety steps to the front door.

"We drove almost seven hours to get here. I'm knocking on the door."

Augustus knocked and knocked and pounded and pounded some more. "Maybe he's not home? We could try -- " The sound of a bolt turning stopped him.

Slowly the door opened, revealing a tall, skinny man pointing a shotgun at us.

"Who are you? And why are you pounding on my door?" He looked angry, but already the shotgun was dropping.

"Sorry to bother you, sir," Augustus said. "We're looking for Peter Van Billy Bob."

"Who are you?"

"I'm Augustus Walters, and this is Hazel Mace. We're fans."

"Fans?"

"Of Peter Van Billy Bob's book, *A Posterior Affliction.*"

"I guess you can come on in." He walked into the, err, I guess it was a house.

"I'll go first," Augustus said.

I followed him into a living room.

"Sir, is Mr. Peter Van Billy Bob here?" I asked.

"He's right here." He tapped his chest.

"Excuse me? You're Peter Van Billy Bob?" I gawked at the man; half his teeth missing. Every inch of his skin red, checkered with scabs and sores.

"Yep." He took out a glass pipe. "Only one there is, as far as I know."

"A crack pipe?" I slapped the side of my head. "You smoke a crack pipe too?"

"Crystal."

"Meth," said Augustus translating.

"Oh, well that's better," I said in disgust.

Augustus sat down on the arm of the couch. "Please, we have some questions about your book, *A Posterior Affliction.*"

"Don't say the name. Don't ever mention that wretched book in front of me." He emptied the contents of a little baggy into the pipe and puffed away.

"Please, we have some questions," Augustus said. "About Anna and her mother."

"They're dead to me. Drop it or leave." He tried burning the pipe again, but it was out.

"Okay, okay." Augustus winked at me and then pulled out his pipe.

Peter Van Billy Bob's eyes widened. "What you got there?"

"Crack cocaine." Augustus pulled out a sandwich-sized Ziploc bag full of little rocks.

"Whoa, boy," Peter Van Billy Bob stuttered. "You could do twenty to life if you got caught with that much Blow."

"Care to help me get rid of it?" Augustus took a long deep drag, not like I'd ever seen him do it before.

50

"Don't mind if I do." Augustus handed the entire bag to him.

He took out the largest rock he could find and puffed away like a dragon.

"So about Anna," Augustus said as casually as he could.

"Sorry, buddy," he spoke between puffs. "It's too personal. She's someone, *was* someone real."

"Wow," Augustus shook his head.

"This is weak Blow." Peter reached into the Ziplock bag for another helping.

"I need the ladies' room," I said, exasperated.

Peter pointed down a hall.

I left Leroy outside, running the tubing under the door.

I didn't really need to use the bathroom, but I had to get out of there. It was such a disappointment. And not just Peter Van Billy Bob—everything. The trip, my life, even Augustus. He was supposed to live so he could remember me, not like my parents, but remember me as a woman. Now he was probably going to die too. It was all just so disappointing.

The toilet needed two flushes Then I put down the lid, which was surprisingly clean, probably because it hadn't been closed in ages. I sat, then put my head in my hands and cried.

After I'd gotten it all out I looked for a tissue, but he had none. No TP either. What he did have was a big stack of letters next to the bowl. The first one was opened; the page torn in half. All that was left was, "…because your book not only inspired me, but helped me to understand what my brother is going through. I hope you can find the time to write him that small note. It would mean so much to him." It was signed, "Your Biggest Fan, Patricia Jones."

I couldn't believe it. As I looked through the sack, most of the letters had been forwarded by his publisher: They were all fan mail!

Chapter 10

The bathroom door was stuck. I forced it open, got Leroy and headed down the hall, grabbing Augustus as I went. "Get your crack and let's go."

"Wait, just a minute," he said, but I pulled him along.

"No, get your drugs. We're going now."

"I don't need them," he said as we headed for the front door. "They're just smashed sugar cubes."

"What? All this time, it wasn't crack?"

"Hell no," he pulled the door open. "You can't light a pipe without smoking it, and I wouldn't smoke crack cocaine—that'd just be stupid."

We were already off balance as we headed out the door. I guess the weight of Augustus, Leroy, and me was too much for the stairs, because they gave way with an enormous crash.

It took us a couple seconds to get up and make sure we weren't hurt. In that time, Peter Van Billy Bob had come over. He looked down at us and said, "The fault, dear children, is not in our stairs, but in ourselves." Then he slammed the door shut.

"Asshole," Augustus said, as I pulled him towards the car.

"What's your deal," he asked as we drove away. "What's wrong?"

"In the bathroom," I cried between sobs. "His fan mail."

"Okay." Augustus was clearly confused.

"He was using it as toilet paper."

"Fan mail? He's using fan mail as toilet paper?" He seemed to think he hadn't understood me. "Well, at least yours wasn't there," he said. "Was it?"

"No, no mine wasn't... Bet he already wiped his ass with it."

We got to the interstate, but I still hadn't stopped crying. Augustus pulled over on the on-ramp and took me in his arms. He started kissing away my tears. He started removing my clothes. I opened up Leroy's valve and kissed him back.

Five minutes later we were done, our bodies wrapped and tangled inside the confined space of his front seat.

"Careful, Hazel," Augustus said as we untangled ourselves. "Careful your tube is stuck on—uh-oh"

"What's that smell?" I plugged my nose despite the fact I hadn't gotten my breath back.

"I think your oxygen tube got caught on my colostomy bag."

I leaned my head out the window for fresh air, but something was wrong—besides the smell. "Oh, no. Leroy is out."

*

Our parents were understandably upset. After the ambulance ride, we both ended up needing a couple days in the hospital. It wasn't till then that I realized just how bad Augustus was. He never told me himself; Isaac had to fill me in. He'd gotten the results back: he was Stage Five-Plus. They loaded him up on pain meds and gave him a couple weeks to live. Turned out our little romp almost killed him.

Not that I regretted it. Don't get me wrong. I would never have ridden that boy had I known he was so sick. But I did, and he didn't die. And now when he was gone, there would be someone to remember him—as a man, if only for a little while. And maybe, I thought, if I write this all down, someone will read it and know what he was really like, my Augustus Walters.

On my way out of the hospital I convinced my parents to let me stop by his room. They rolled me in, but wouldn't leave us alone—probably afraid I'd jump his bones.

"Hey, Gus. How you feeling?" I asked in a small voice.

"Good. Good." His reply was even smaller. "They'd let me out of here, but my parents are being over cautious." He stayed in the hospital for another week.

Chapter 11

That day we spent together was Gus' last good day. I don't think his parents ever forgave me. Augustus wanted us to throw a going away party for him where he'd invite all his friends to come and take turns roasting him. But his parents wouldn't go for it. In fact, when he was really sick, they wouldn't even let me see him. Gus died three days after I last saw him, and I didn't find out he was gone until the day after he passed. Those four days were actually worse than what came after.

I was pissed at his parents. But I knew I couldn't understand what they were going through, so I let it slide. Besides, only I knew the real Gus. The man who liked porn and animal balloons and who stood by his friend's side no matter what. Only I knew the man he would have become.

It was a couple weeks later when I got a call from Gus's Mom. She said they were going through his bag of stuff from the hospital and found a folded up note addressed to me. They asked me if I wanted to come by and pick it up. I made my mom stop dinner and drive me over immediately.

I didn't read it in the car. I waited until we got home. My mom helped me get Leroy upstairs (at that point, I normally stayed downstairs until Dad got home). I closed the door and sat on the bed to read my note.

It was written in blue Sharpie. I suspected it was the one the hospital used to write his vitals on the whiteboard in his room. The letters were rough and jaded.

Hazel,

After you went to the bathroom, I got Peter The Asshole to start talking. Not about Anna, but about her mother.

Turns out her mother got arrested on drug charges, even though she wasn't selling. Her stuff was just too potent. But the cops didn't care about her, and she got a deal by helping them get the Arab Oil

Barron—who, it turned out, was really into human trafficking. He

was sentenced to a life term in Federal prison.

After her probation, she moved to California where she could

grow pot without interference from the law. While there she met and

married a guy who sold specialty seeds (the non-drug kind) over the

Internet.

They lived happily ever after—I wish we could too.

I couldn't believe it. Literally, I wasn't sure if he had just made it

all up, but I didn't care. Even if it wasn't Peter Van Billy Bob's

story, he couldn't have done it any better. That letter was all I had

from Augustus Walters, but it was enough.

* * *

About The Author:

Adam Aarons grew up in the slums of Bavaria, where he survived by selling Adult videocassettes to tourists before being adopted by Catholic missionaries. After escaping, he joined the Church of Scientology's literacy program and learned to write science fiction. He currently lives in LA with three beagles, two cats, and a turtle.

7215228R00043

Printed in Great Britain
by Amazon.co.uk, Ltd.,
Marston Gate.